THIRD EDITION

3

LET'S GO

WORKBOOK

Elaine Cross

Ritsuka Nakata

Karen Frazier

Barbara Hoskins

OXFORD
UNIVERSITY PRESS

Let's Start

A. Write and connect.

| have | some | do | don't | you | want | Thanks |

1. Oh, no! I <u>don't</u> have any potato chips. •

2. Really? Do _____? •

3. Sure. Do you want _____ grapes? •

• a. Yes, I _____. Do you _____ some?

• b. Yes, please. _____!

• c. I think I _____ some.

B. Unscramble and write the words.

1. etsapnu = _____peanuts_____

2. arccresk = _____

3. yacdn = _____

4. norcopp = _____

C. Look and write.

I have some candy.

I don't have any candy.

1. _____

2. _____

3. _____.

4. _____.

D. Write and connect.

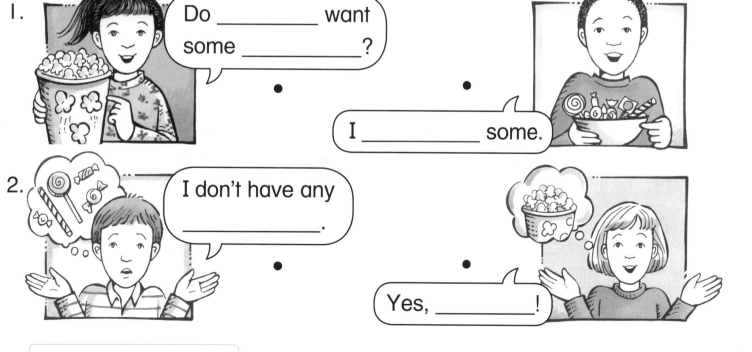

1. Do _____ want some _____?

I _____ some.

2. I don't have any _____.

Yes, _____!

Let's Learn _____

A. Look and write.

Down

1.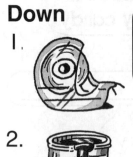

2.

4.

5.

| chalk | paint | glue | string |
| tape | scissors | paper | ribbon |

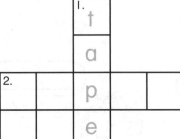

Across

2.
3.
6.
7.

B. Write sentences.

1.  She has some chalk.

2. He doesn't have any _____.

3.  _____.

4.  _____.

C. Answer the questions.

1.

What does he have?

_____.

2.

What does she have?

_____.

3.

_____?

_____.

4.

_____?

_____.

D. Read and match.

1.  Does he have any string? •

2.  Does she have any paper? •

3.  Does she have any paint? •

4. Does he have any chalk? •

• Yes, he does.

• No, she doesn't.

• Yes, she does.

• No, he doesn't.

Let's Learn More

A. Look and write.

1.

magnets

2.

_____

3.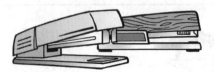

_____

4.

_____

5.

_____

6.

_____

7.

_____

8.

_____

> calculators
> scissors
> colored pencils
> rubber bands
> magnets
> push pins
> paint brushes
> staplers

B. Complete the sentences.

1.

They have some magnets.
They don't have any staplers.

2.

_____ scissors.
_____ rubberbands.

3.

_____ paint brushes.
_____ push pins.

C. Write the questions or answers.

What do they have?

They have some push pins.

1.

What do they have?

_____.

2.

_____?

They have some scissors.

3.

_____?

They have some magnets.

D. Read and circle.

1. Do they have any colored pencils?

Yes, they do.
No, they don't.

2. Do they have any push pins?

Yes, they do.
No, they don't.

3. Do they have any magnets?

Yes, they do.
No, they don't.

4. Do they have any rubber bands?

Yes, they do.
No, they don't.

Let's Build

A. Write sentences.

1.

He wants some cake.
He doesn't want any stew.

cake
scissors
stew
ribbon
cookies
crackers

2.

_____.
_____.

3.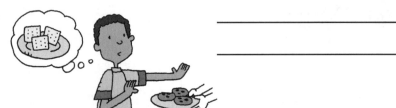

_____.
_____.

B. Read and circle.

1.

Do you want some stew?
  (Yes, please.)
  No, thank you.

2.

Do you want some cake?
  Yes, please.
  No, thank you.

3.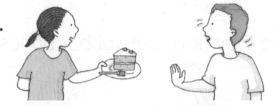

Do you want some cookies?
  Yes, please.
  No, thank you.

Let's Read

A. Read and write.

1. Emma has a new CD. She _____ a CD player.

2. Anna _____ a CD player.

3. They can _____ the _____ and the CD.

has	CD player
doesn't have	share

B. What about you? Write.

I have some cake.

I want some cake.

some ice cream
some popcorn
some paint
a new CD
a calculator

1. What do you have?

   I have _____.

2. What do you want?

   I want _____.

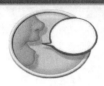 ## Let's Start

A. Read and number.

1	Excuse me. Where's the office?
☐	OK.
☐	I'm going there now. Come with me.
☐	Thanks for your help.
☐	You're welcome.
☐	It's next to the gym.

B. Write the rooms.

music room	science room	art room	classroom
lunchroom	gym	office	library

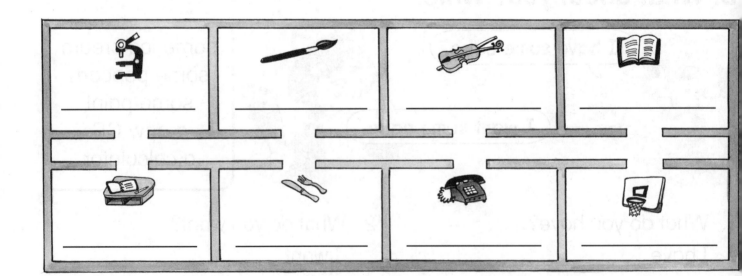

C. Look and write.

next to   across from   between

1.

_____

2.

_____

3.

_____

D. Look and write.

1.

Where's the library?

It's <u>next to the art room</u>.

2.

Where's the science room?

It's _____ the _____.

3.

Where's the classroom?

It's _____ the _____

_____ and the _____.

4.

Where's the office?

_____

_____.

Let's Learn _____

A. Look, read, and match.

1.

- in the computer lab •
- in the restroom •
- in the pool •
- in the nurse's office •
- on the stairs •
- in the auditorium •

2.

3.

4.

5.

6.

B. Read and write in the chart.

1. She was in the pool this morning.
   She is in the auditorium now.

2. He is on the stairs now.
   He was in the restroom this morning.

3. He was in the hallway this morning.
   He is on the playground now.

This morning	in the pool	_____	_____
Now	in the auditorium	_____	_____

C. Look, read, and match.

1.

2.

3.

4.

Where was she this morning? •

Where is she now? •

Where was he this morning? •

Where is he now? •

• He was in the computer lab.

• She is on the playground.

• He is in the pool.

• She was in the auditorium.

D. Read and check.

1. Is she in the nurse's office now?
   No, she isn't.

2. Was he on the stairs this morning?
   Yes, he was.

3. Was he in the computer lab this morning?   No, he wasn't.

4. Is she in the restroom now?
   No, she isn't.

Let's Learn More

A. Look, read, and match.

1.

2.

3.

- at the bakery •
- at the clinic •
- at the factory •
- at the repair shop •
- at the airport •
- at the bus stop •

4.

5.

6.

B. Read, number, and write.

8:45 AM   8:30 AM   BAKERY   BOOKS   5:45 PM

SALE   Now   BUS STOP

Yesterday....

1. They were at the bookstore __at 5:45 p.m._____ .

2. They were at the train station _____ .

3. They were at the bakery _____ .

4. Where are they now? _____ .

C. Answer the questions.

1.

   Where were they yesterday?

   They were _____ .

2.

   Where are they now?

   They are _____ .

3.

   Where are they now?

   _____ .

4.

   Where were they yesterday?

   _____ .

D. Look at C. Write the questions and answers.

1.

   Are they at the train station now?

   _____ .

2.

   Were they at the factory yesterday?

   _____ .

3.

   _____ bookstore now?

   _____ . They _____ .

4.

   _____ bakery yesterday?

   _____ . They _____ .

 # Let's Build

A. Look and write.

| rainy | sunny | snowy | windy | cloudy |

Yesterday   Today

1. <u>It was sunny yesterday</u>.

2. _____ today.

3. _____ .

4. _____ .

5. _____ .

B. Write the questions and answers.

1.

How was the weather yesterday?

_____ .

2.

How is the weather today?

_____ .

3.

_____ ?

_____ .

4.

_____ ?

_____ .

 # Let's Read

A. Read and match.

1. This is now a big frog. •

2. It was a little tadpole. •

3. It was a caterpillar. •

4. This is now a black and gray butterfly. •

a.

b

c.

d.

B. Answer the questions.

1. What was the butterfly?

   It was _____.

2. What is it now?

   _____.

3. What was the frog?

   _____.

4. Is it a frog now?

   _____.

✓

Units 1-2 Listen and Review

A. Write the questions or answers.

1.

Yesterday Today

Where is she now?

_____.

Where was she yesterday?

_____.

2.

This morning Now GATE 47

_____?

They're at the airport.

_____?

They were at the bus stop.

3.

Does he have any glue?

_____.

What does he have?

_____.

4.

_____?

No, thank you.

_____?

Yes, please!

Where were they yesterday?

_____.

Where are they now?

_____.

Do they have any scissors?

_____.

Do they have any colored pencils?

_____.

5.

Yesterday

Today

A. Write

> geography   laptop computer   online

1.

_____

2.

_____

3.

_____

B. Change the sentences.

> I ⟶ he   we ⟶ they   live ⟶ lives   my ⟶ his/her

1. My name is Tony. ⟶ <u>His name is Tony</u>.

2. I live in the United States. ⟶ He _____.

3. I go to a small school. ⟶ _____.

4. We study English, science, and geography. ⟶ _____

_____.

C. Answer the questions.

1. What is his name?

_____.

2. Does he go to a big school?

_____.

3. What does he study?

_____.

4. Where does he live?

_____.

✓

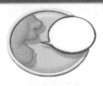 **Let's Start**

A. Read and write.

Really? So do I!
I live on the fifth floor.
Where does she live?

1.

   I'm going to my grandmothers's house today.

   _____.

2.

   She lives in that apartment building.

   _____.

3.

   _____.

   My grandmother lives on the second floor.

B. Write.

| sixth | fourth | first | ninth | fifth |
| third | eighth | seventh | tenth | second |

10 __tenth__   8 _____   6 _____   4 _____   2 _____

9 _____   7 _____   5 _____   3 _____   1 _____

C. Complete the sentences.

1.  She lives on the _____ floor.

2.  He _____ _____.

3.  She _____ _____.

4.  He _____ _____.

Let's Learn

A. Look and write.

a bedroom	a bathroom	a kitchen
a living room	a garage	an entryway

<u>a bedroom</u>   _____   _____

This is my house.

_____   _____   _____

B. Look at A. Write sentences.

1. <u>There is a garage in my house</u> _____.

2. <u>There are two bathrooms in</u> _____.

3. _____ three _____ on the second floor _____.

4. _____ a living room _____ house _____.

5. <u>The garage is on</u> _____ floor _____.

C. Complete the questions and answers.

Yes, there is.   No, there isn't.

1. <u>Is there</u> a dining room <u>in her house</u>?
   <u>Yes, there is</u>.

2. _____ a basement _____?
   _____.

3. _____ an entryway _____?
   _____.

4. _____ a kitchen _____?
   _____.

D. Look and write.

1.

There were three chairs in our bedroom. Now there aren't any chairs in our bedroom.

2.

<u>There were   in</u>
<u>our entryway. Now</u>
_____
_____.

3.

_____
_____
_____
_____.

Let's Learn More _____

A. Write.

> a skateboard   a unicycle   skis   in-line skates
> a scooter   a sled   a snowboard   ice skates

1.  _____

2.  _____

3.  _____

4.  _____

5.  _____

6.  _____

7.  _____

8. 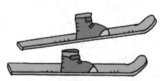 _____

B. Write sentences.

The scooter is in the garage.

The in-line skates are in the entryway.

1.  _____
_____.

2. 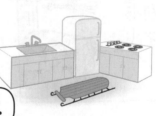 _____
_____.

C. Complete the questions and answers.

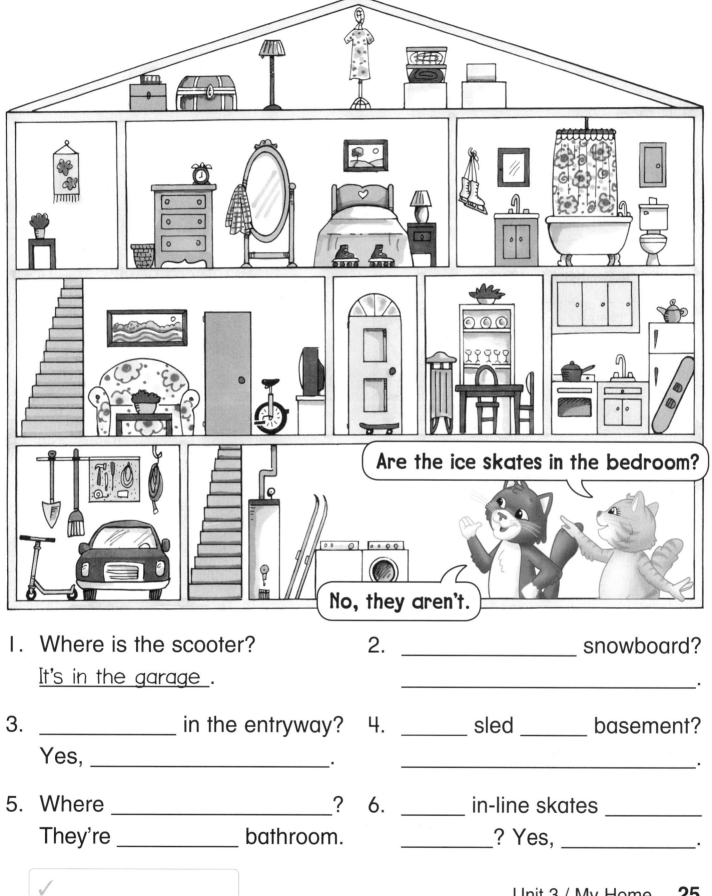

Are the ice skates in the bedroom?

No, they aren't.

1. Where is the scooter?
   It's in the _garage_ .

2. _____ snowboard?
   _____.

3. _____ in the entryway?
   Yes, _____.

4. _____ sled _____ basement?
   _____.

5. Where _____?
   They're _____ bathroom.

6. _____ in-line skates _____
   _____? Yes, _____.

Let's Build

A. Write and draw.

1. The books were <u>under the bed</u>. Now they're on the desk.

2. The ice skates were _____. Now they're behind the door.

3. The snowboard was _____. Now it's under the bed.

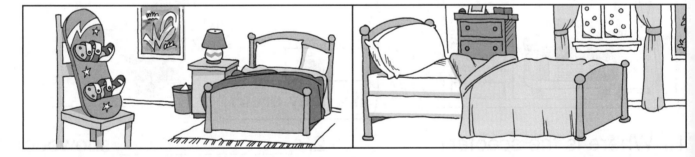

4. The bag was _____. Now it's next to the bed.

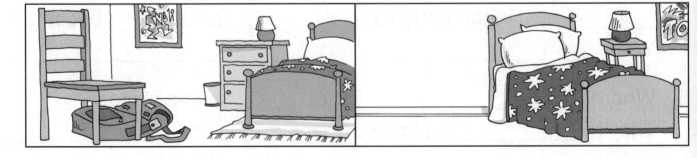

Let's Read

A. Read and circle.

1. Brett ⟨likes⟩ / lives books.

2. Brett has / walks a lot of books in his house.

3. His books are / am in the living room.

4. His books is / are in the kitchen. His books are everywhere.

5. Brett reads / walks books every day.

B. Read and match.

1. What does Brett like? •

2. What does Brett do every day? •

3. Where are Brett's books? •

• His books are in the living room and kitchen.

• He likes books.

• He reads books every day.

C. What about you? Write and draw.

What do you like?

_____

_____

_____.

✓

Let's Start

A. Read and circle.

1. Which hat do you like?

(I like the plaid one.)

It's a plaid hat.

2. Which one is the same?

   Is this one the same?

No, it's different.

3. What about this one?

There is a hat
on the chair.

Yes, it's the same.

B. Look and check.

1.

☐ the same
☑ different

2.

☐ the same
☐ different

3.

☐ the same
☐ different

4.

☐ the same
☐ different

C. Read and match.

1.  (I like the plaid one.) •

a.
•

2.  (I like the striped one.) •

b.
•

3.  (I like the polka dot one.) •

c.
•

4.  (I like the checked one.) •

d.
•

D. What about you? Which one do you like?

| little | old | new | striped | big | polka dot |

1. I like the _____ one.

2. _____.

3. _____.

✓

Let's Learn

A. Look and check. What are they wearing?

Lisa
Meg

Chris
Stan

	Lisa	Chris	Meg	Stan
blouse	✓			
skirt	✓			
dress				
shirt				
pants				
shorts				
shoes	✓			
socks	✓			

B. Look at A. Write sentences.

1. She's wearing a skirt . She's not wearing pants .

2. _____ . _____ .

3. _____ . _____ .

4. _____ . _____ .

C. Write the questions and answers.

What's he wearing?

He's wearing a shirt, pants, and shoes.

1. What's he wearing?

He's _____

_____

_____ .

2. What's she wearing?

She's _____

_____

_____ .

3. What's _____?

_____

_____

_____ .

4. _____?

_____

_____

_____ .

5. _____?

_____

_____

_____ .

6. _____?

_____

_____

_____ .

Let's Learn More _____

A. Write sentences.

slippers	pajamas	jacket	T-shirt
sweatshirt	sweater	boots	jeans

1. These are my boots.

2. This is my _____ _____.

3. _____ _____.

4. _____ _____.

5. _____ _____.

6. _____ _____.

7. _____ _____.

8. _____ _____.

B. Connect and write.

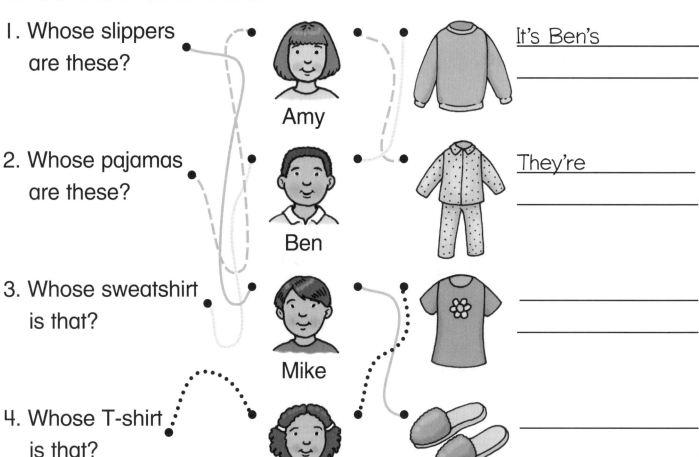

1. Whose slippers are these?

   It's Ben's _____.

2. Whose pajamas are these?

   They're _____.

3. Whose sweatshirt is that?

   _____.

4. Whose T-shirt is that?

   _____.

Amy

Ben

Mike

Kayla

C. Look and write.

John   Rachel

1. Is this Rachel's jacket?

   Yes, it is _____.

2. Is this Rachel's T-shirt?

   _____.

3. Are these John's shoes?

   _____.

4. Are these Rachel's slippers?

   _____.

Let's Build

A. Read and circle.

1.
She's wearing a (big,) white little, (black) sweater.

2.
He's wearing old, long new, short jeans.

3.
She's wearing a long, striped short, polka dot dress.

B. Write sentences.

| little | long | polka dot | T-shirt | pajamas | boots |
| big | white | striped | new | plaid | hat |

1.
She's wearing long, plaid pajamas.

2.
_____
_____.

3.
_____
_____.

4.
_____
_____.

 **Let's Read** _____

A. Read and write the words.

1.

Jessica wears a _____
to _____ every day.

jeans
school
different
polka dot
sweater
uniform
pajamas

2.

After school, she wears the
same _____
and _____.

3.

She wears _____ _____ every night.
Tonight she is wearing her new
_____ pajamas.

B. Answer the questions.

1. What does Jessica wear to school every day?
   She wears _____ to school every day.

2. What do you wear to school every day?
   I wear _____ to school every day.

3. What does Jessica wear after school?
   She wears _____.

4. What do you wear after school?
   I wear _____.

Units 3-4   Listen and Review

A. Answer the questions.

Emily's bedroom	Matthew's bedroom

1. Where is Emily's snowboard?

    _____.

2. Is Matthew's cat next to the TV?

    _____.

3. Is Matthew wearing pants?

    _____.

4. Where are the books?

    _____.

5. What is Emily wearing?

    _____.

6. Whose ice skates are these?

    _____.

B. Answer the questions.

Yesterday   Today

1. Where were the in-line skates yesterday?

    _____.

2. Where is the sled now?

    _____.

A. Read, number, and match.

☐ I live in New Zealand. •

a. •

☐ We like to go to the beach. •

b. •

☐ 1 My name is Megan. •

c. •

☐ My brother and I go to
the same school. •

d. •

B. Match questions and answers.

1. What is her name? •

• Megan lives in
New Zealand.

2. Who goes to Megan's school? •

• Megan's brother goes
to Megan's school.

3. What does Megan like? •

• Her name is Megan.

4. Where does Megan live? •

• Megan likes the beach.

✓

 ## Let's Start

A. Read, look, and match.

1. This is going to be fun. •

• Yes, I do. It's in my bag. •

 •

2. What time does the train leave? •

• I can't wait. •

 •

3. Do you have your bathing suit? •

• It leaves at 9:15. •

 •

B. Write.

It's 11:35.

BUS STOP

It's 11:36!

1. It's _____. 2. _____. 3. _____. 4. _____.

C. Look and circle.

1.
a train
(a bus)

2.
an airplane
a train

3.
a boat
an airplane

4.
a boat
a bus

D. Unscramble the questions and write the answers.

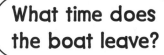
What time does the boat leave?

BOAT
12:15

It leaves at 12:15.

1. time What train does leave the
   What time does _____?
   _____.

2. does plane What the time leave
   _____?
   _____.

3. boat leave does What the time
   _____?
   _____.

4. leave time What the does bus
   _____?
   _____.

✓

Let's Learn

A. Write.

> take a taxi
> take a train
> walk
> ride a bicycle

1.

_____

2.

_____

3.

_____

4.

_____

B. Circle.

1.

I take a subway / take a taxi to school.

2.

I take a bus / ride a bicycle to school.

3.

I ride a bicycle / walk to school.

4.

I take a bus / take a train to school.

C. Write sentences.

	Mon	Tues	Wed	Thurs	Fri
(boy)	bus	bus	bus	bus	bus
(girl)	bicycle	bicycle	bicycle	bicycle	bicycle

1. I _____ bus to school.

2. I _____ train _____.

3. I _____ taxi _____.

4. I _____ bicycle _____.

D. Connect and write.

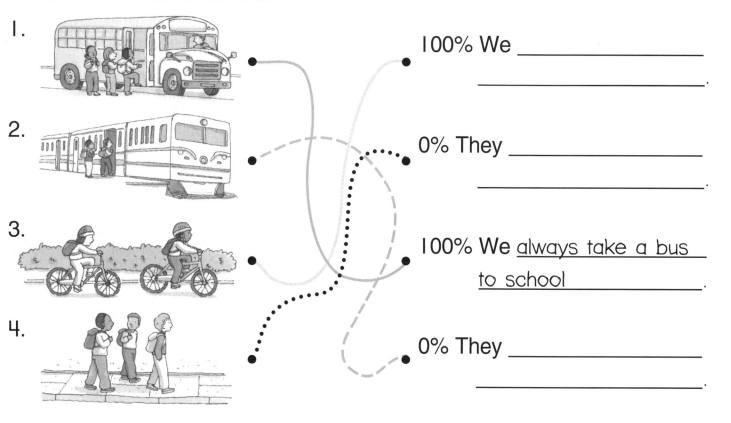

1.

100% We _____ _____.

2.

0% They _____ _____.

3.

100% We <u>always take a bus</u> <u>to school</u>.

4.

0% They _____ _____.

✓

Let's Learn More

A. Read and match.

1. drive a tractor •

2. fly an airplane •

3. fly a helicopter •

4. drive a police car •

5. drive a truck •

6. drive a car •

B. Write two sentences.

> 80% = usually   40% = sometimes

1.  **80%**  **40%**

He usually drives a tractor at work.
He sometimes drives a truck at work.

2.  **80%**  **40%**

_____
_____ .

3.   **80%**  **40%**

_____ .
_____ .

4.   **80%**  **40%**

_____ .
_____ .

C. Look at B. Write the questions and answers.

Does she ever drive a car at work?

Yes, she does.

1.  Does he ever
fly an airplane
at work?

_____

_____.

2.  Does she ever
ride a motorcycle
at work?

_____

_____.

3.  _____

_____

fire engine _____

_____?

_____.

4.  _____

_____ tractor

_____?

_____

_____.

D. Read and number.

1. She usually takes a bus to work.
2. She usually drives a car to work.
3. Sometimes she rides a scooter.
4. Sometimes she rides a motorcycle.

 80%

 40%

 80%

 40%

✓

Let's Build

A. Read and circle.

| 100% = always | 80% = usually | 40% = sometimes | 0% = never |

1. He usually watches TV at home.

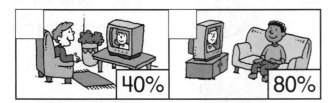
40%   80%

2. She never talks on the telephone at school.

0%   100%

3. She always does homework in the library.

40%   100%

4. He sometimes plays baseball in the park.

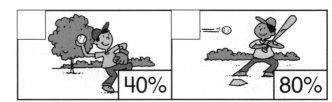
40%   80%

B. Write sentences.

| at school | speak English | at home | do homework |

1.

0%

She never sings
a song at the
zoo.

2.

80%

_____
_____
_____ .

3.

100%

_____
_____
_____ .

Let's Read

A. Read and match.

Mrs. Jones always goes to work in the morning. She is a teacher. She usually stands up. She sometimes sits down. She never eats in the classroom. • •

Mr. Brown always goes to work in the afternoon. He usually drives a truck. He sometimes drinks tea at work. He never drinks soda. • •

B. Look at A and write in the chart.

always	He always goes to work in the afternoon.	
sometimes		
never		
usually		

✓

Let's Start

A. Unscramble and write.

1.

Hi, Kate. Where are you going?

today the going I'm library to

_____

_____.

2.

How about you? Are you going home?

to the No not I'm park going I'm

_____

_____.

3.

Have fun.

Thanks later you See

_____

_____

B. Write.

Have _____.

MOVIES

NOW SHOWING THE MOUSE

Thanks. _____.

C. Write.

| an amusement park | a water park | a concert | a movie |

1. I'm going to _____
   _____.

2. _____
   _____.

3. _____
   _____.

4. _____
   _____.

D. Write the questions and answers.

1. Where are you
   going?
   I'm going to an
   amusement park.

2. Where _____
   _____?
   I'm _____
   _____.

3. _____
   _____?
   _____
   _____.

4. _____
   _____?
   _____
   _____.

Let's Learn

A. Look and write.

| go to a pet store | go bowling | go shopping | watch movies |
| play with friends | clean my room | sleep late | stay home |

1.

_____

2.

_____

3.

_____

4.

_____

5.

_____

6.

_____

7.

_____

8.

_____

B. Write.

I		She/He
1. go	→	goes
2. watch	→	_____
3. _____	→	cleans
4. sleep	→	_____
5. _____	→	stays

C. Write sentences.

> 100% = always   80% = usually   40% = sometimes   0% = never

1.

   I never clean my room on the
   weekend.

2.

   _____

   _____.

3.

   _____

   _____.

4.

   _____

   _____.

D. Look at C. Write the questions and answers.

1. What does she do on the weekend?

   She never cleans her room _____.

2. What _____ on the weekend?

   She _____.

3. What _____?

   He _____.

4. _____?

   _____.

Let's Learn More _____

A. Write.

I/You/We/They		He/She
1. practice karate	→	<u>practices karate</u> _____
2. do homework	→	_____
3. study English	→	_____
4. play tennis	→	_____
5. read e-mail	→	_____

B. Unscramble, write, and match.

1. ctaecpri rakaet

   _____

2. ylap sinten

   _____

3. dusty glEnhis

   _____

4. od mowhoker

   _____

a.

b.

c.

d.

C. Complete the sentences.

1. She usually _____ tennis after school.

2. He sometimes _____ homework after school.

3. We always _____ English after school.

D. Answer the questions.

1. When does she read e-mail?
   always/before
   <u>She always reads e-mail</u>
   <u>before school</u> .

2. When does he practice karate?
   usually/after
   _____
   _____ .

3. When does she do gymnastics?
   always/after
   _____
   _____ .

4. When does he play tennis?
   usually/before
   _____
   _____ .

E. Answer the questions.

	before school	after school
	study English read e-mail	play tennis do homework
	do gymnastics read e-mail	do homework practice karate

1. Does he ever read e-mail after school?
   <u>No, he doesn't</u> .

2. Does she ever read e-mail before school?
   _____ .

3. Does she ever do gymnastics after school?
   _____ .

4. Does he ever study English before school?
   _____ .

 # Let's Build

A. Write and circle.

1. He _____ 2. They _____ 3. She _____

_____ _____ _____

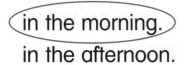

in the morning. in the afternoon. on Saturdays.
in the afternoon. in the evening. on Sundays.

B. Write sentences.

1.  When does he study English?

100%: <u>He always studies English in the morning.</u>
40%: _____ in the afternoon.

2.  When do they do homework?

80%: _____.
0%: _____ in the morning.

3. When does she go shopping?

100%: _____.
40%: _____ on Tuesdays.

Let's Read

A. Write and match.

| swim practice | 6:00 | free | After | busy |

Molly is a _____ girl.

1. She leaves every morning at _____ a.m. •

2. Before school, she goes to _____ _____. •

3. _____ school, she studies English. •

4. On Sundays, she's _____. Usually she stays home. •

B. Complete the sentences.

What about you?

1. I _____ my house every morning at _____.

2. Before school, I _____.

3. After school, I _____.

4. On _____, I'm free.

Units 5-6 Listen and Review

A. Match.

1. Does she ever walk to school? •   • He cleans his room
                                        on the weekend.

2. When do they practice karate? •

                                    • Yes, they do.

3. What does he do on the weekend? •

                                    • Yes, she does.

4. Does he ever drive a
   fire engine at work? •

                                    • They usually practice
                                      karate in the afternoon.

5. Do they ever do homework
   before school? •

                                    • No, he doesn't.

B. Write.

1. She sometimes _____ bowling on Saturdays.

2. I always _____ tennis after school.

3. They usually _____ homework in the evening.

4. We always _____ a bus to school.

5. He never _____ an airplane at work.

6. I'm _____ to a concert.

A. Write.

| fiddle | dance | harp | accordion |

1.

2.

3.

4.

_____   _____   _____   _____

B. Read and answer.

My name is Kevin. My family lives in Ireland. We like music. We practice every day. My sister dances.

1. Who dances?
   His _____.

2. Who likes music?
   _____.

3. When do they practice?

   _____.

4. Where do they live?

   _____.

C. Write.

1. his father/accordion
   His father plays the accordion.

2. his mother/harp

   _____.

3. he/fiddle

   _____.

4. my sister/dance

   _____.

 ## Let's Start

A. Read and number.

☐ My mothers's an office worker.

☐ Oh. What does an office worker do?

1 What does your father do?

☐ He's a pilot.

☐ I'm not sure.

B. Look and write.

1.
My mother is a zoo keeper.

2. _____.

3. _____.

4. _____.

C. Write the questions and answers.

What does your mother do?

She's a pilot.

1. What does your father do?

2. What does your _____?

He's a baseball player.

_____.

3. What _____?

4. _____?

She's _____.

_____.

D. What about you? Write.

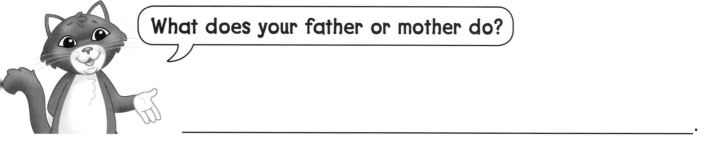

What does your father or mother do?

_____.

Let's Learn

A. Look, unscramble and write.

| photographer | factory worker | fisherman |
| veterinarian | sales clerk | mechanic |

1. annaretievir

He's a veterinarian_____.

2. othopergharp

She's_____.

3. seclerakls

_____.

4. hisner fam

_____.

5. cortyfa krewor

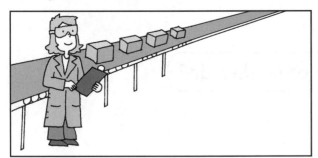

_____.

6. chicanem

_____.

B. Write and match.

What's her job?

She's a salesclerk.

SALE

1. What's his job? •

She's _____ _____.

2. What's _____ ? •

He's _____ _____.

3. _____ ? •

He's _____ a _____ mechanic _____.

4. _____ ? •

_____ _____.

5. _____ ? •

_____ _____.

6. _____ ? •

_____ _____.

Let's Learn More _____

A. Write the words.

I/You/We/They	She/He
1. catch fish	catches fish
2.	fixes cars
3. help animals	
4.	makes things
5. take pictures	
6.	sells things

B. Read and write.

A veterinarian helps animals.

1.

A _____ helps animals.

2.

A salesclerk _____.

3.

A _____.

4.

A fisherman _____.

C. Write the questions and answers.

1. What does _____ do?
   _____ makes things.

2. What does a mechanic do?
   _____.

3. What _____?
   _____.

4. _____?
   _____.

5. _____?
   _____.

6. _____?
   _____.

What does a cat do?

11:00 a.m.

A cat sleeps late!

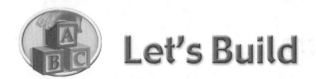

Let's Build

A. Read, look, and write.

1. I work in a store. I sell things. What's my job?

   You're a _____.

2. I wear a uniform. I fly airplanes. What's my job?

   _____.

3. I wear a uniform. I drive a fire engine. What's my job?

   _____.

4. I work on a boat. I catch fish. What's my job?

   _____.

5. I work in a garage. I fix cars. What's my job?

   _____.

Let's Read

A. Read and connect.

Maya is a photographer. She takes pictures every day. Sometimes she takes pictures of lions.

Jeff is a fisherman. He catches fish every day. Sometimes he sells fish on the weekend.

Liz is a baker. She bakes bread every day. Sometimes she bakes cakes for birthdays.

Maya	Liz	Jeff
•	•	•
•	•	•
fisherman	photographer	baker
•	•	•
•	•	•
bakes bread	takes pictures	catches fish
•	•	•
•	•	•
takes pictures of lions	sells fish	bakes cakes

 **Let's Start**

A. Number the sentences.

☐ I like soccer more.

☐ Yes, I do.

☐ I like football and soccer.

☐ Which sport do you like more?

☐ Which sports do you like?

☐ I like soccer, too.

☐ I Do you like sports?

B. Read and match.

1. football •

2. track •

3. basketball •

4. volleyball •

5. soccer •

6. baseball •

• a.

• b.

• c.

• d.

• e.

• f.

C. Write sentences.

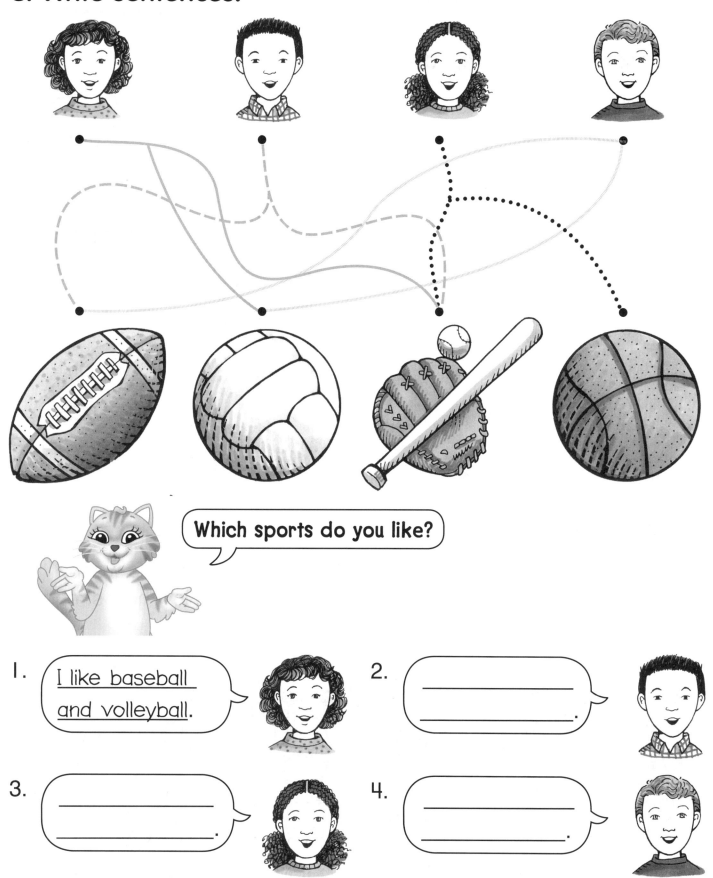

Which sports do you like?

1. I like baseball and volleyball.

2. _____ .

3. _____ .

4. _____ .

Let's Learn

A. Unscramble, write, and match.

1. lamsl _____ •

2. grostn _____ •

3. glith _____ •

4. akwe _____ •

5. yahve _____ •

6. staf _____ •

a. •

b. •

c. •

d. •

e. •

f. •

B. Read and match.

1. She was slow.
   Now she's fast.
   •
   •

2. He was light.
   Now he's heavy.
   •
   •

3. He was weak.
   Now he's strong.
   •
   •

a.

b.

c.

C. Look and circle.

1. Is he small?

(Yes, he is.)
No, he isn't.

2. Was she strong?

Yes, she was.
No, she wasn't.

3. Was he slow?

Yes, he was.
No, he wasn't.

4. Is she heavy?

Yes, she is.
No, she isn't.

D. Look and write.

1.

They were slow. Now they're fast.

2.

_____.

3.

_____.

4.

_____.

Let's Learn More

A. Number.

1. a swimmer

2. a baseball player

3. a volleyball player

4. a runner

5. a gymnast

6. a football player

☐ ☐ ☐ ☐ ☐ ☐

B. Complete the sentences.

1. The runner is fast. The runner is <u>faster</u>
   <u>than the volleyball player</u>.
   The volleyball player is small. The
   volleyball player is <u>smaller than the runner</u>.

2. The football player is heavy. The football
   player is _____.
   The gymnast is short. The gymnast is
   _____.

3. The baseball player is big. The baseball
   player is _____.
   The swimmer is strong. The swimmer
   is _____.

C. Look and write.

1.

Who is stronger _____?

The gymnast is stronger _____.

2.

_____?

_____.

3.

_____?

_____.

4.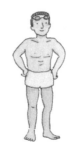

_____?

_____.

D. Read, look, and check.

1. Is the football player stronger than the swimmer?

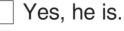 Yes, he is.

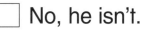 No, he isn't.

2. Is the runner lighter than the gymnast?

Yes, she is.

No, she isn't.

3. Is the baseball player bigger than the football player?

Yes, he is.

No, he isn't.

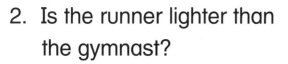

Let's Build

A. Read and write.

1. The refrigerator is bigger than the TV.

   The TV is smaller

   _____ .

2. The car is heavier than the bicycle.

   _____

   _____ .

3. The helicopter is slower than the airplane.

   _____

   _____ .

4. The calculator is smaller than the skateboard.

   _____

   _____ .

B. Answer the questions.

1. Which one is lighter, the tiger or the cat?

   The cat is lighter than the tiger.

2. Which one is taller, the man or the boy?

   _____ .

3. Which one is faster, the car or the skateboard?

   _____ .

4. Which one is thinner, the flower or the tree?

   _____ .

   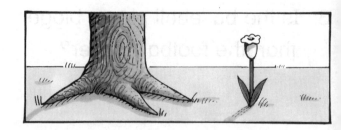

Let's Read

A. Read and write.

Jim is a skier. He likes _____. He was short
and _____. Now he's _____ and strong.
He is _____ than the other skiers, too. Someday,
Jim _____ to be in the Winter Games.

weak
small
fast
faster
than
Someday
wants
tall
skiing

Suzie is a speed skater. She was _____ and
slow. Now she's big and _____. She is faster
_____ the other skaters. _____,
Suzie wants to be in the Winter Games.

B. Match the questions and answers.

1. What does Jim like? •

2. Was Suzie fast? •

3. Is Jim tall? •

4. Do Jim and Suzie want to
   be in the Winter Games? •

• No, she wasn't.

• He likes skiing.

• Yes, he is.

• Yes, they do.

Units 7-8 Listen and Review

A. Read and match.

1. The volleyball player is taller than the football player.

2. I like soccer and track.

3. My mother's an office worker.

4. She was small. Now she's big.

a.

b.

c.

d.

B. Write the questions or answers.

1. Which is bigger, the tiger or the cat?

   _____.

2. _____?

   She's a mechanic.

3. What does your father do?

   _____.

4. _____?

   A fisherman catches fish.

Melissa

A. Read and write.

My _____ is Melissa. I live in _____. My _____
is a _____. She helps tourists. Sometimes I _____
my mother. I _____ tourists, too.

help
like
Canada
name
mother
tour guide

B. Read and connect.

1. Where does Melissa live? •

2. What does her mother do? •

3. What does a tour guide do? •

4. What does Melissa sometimes do? •

5. What does Melissa like? •

• She's a tour guide.

• She lives in Canada.

• A tour guide helps tourists.

• Sometimes she helps her mother.

• She likes tourists.

✓

My Desk _____

A. Look and write.

stapler
scissors
paper
paint
magnets
calculator
paint brushes
rubber bands

1. They have a stapler.

2. They have some _____.

3. They don't have any _____.

4. _____.

5. _____.

6. _____.

7. _____.

8. _____.

B. Draw and write.

What about you?

What do you have in your desk?

I have _____ and

_____.

I don't have any _____

or _____.

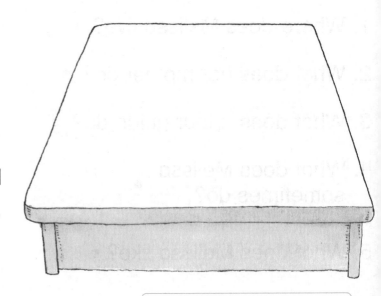

Who Was First?

A. Write the names.

Ann | Ben | Sue | Ken | Tom | Ron | Ray | Tim

Judy | Amy | Tina

| tenth | sixth | first | third | eighth |
| fourth | second | ninth | fifth | seventh |

1. Who was first? Ann.

2. Who was third? _____.

3. Who was second? _____.

4. Who was ninth? _____.

5. Who was tenth? _____.

6. Who was seventh? _____.

7. Who was fifth? _____.

8. Who was eighth? _____.

9. Who was sixth? _____.

10. Who was fourth? _____.

My School

A. Read and label the rooms.

The pool is next to the gym.

The music room is across from the gym.

The office is between the library and the art room.

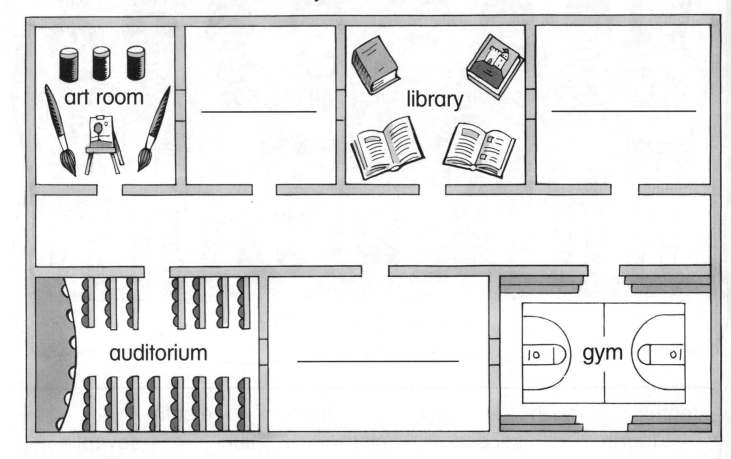

B. Write.

What about your school?

What rooms does your school have?

My school has a _____

and a _____.

It doesn't have a _____.

The Weather

A. Read and write.

It was windy yesterday.
It was windy on Thursday, too.
It was cloudy on Wednesday.
It was rainy on Monday and Tuesday.
It was snowy on Sunday.
But, it's sunny today!

Sun	Mon	Tues	Wed	Thur	Fri	Sat
_____	rainy	_____	_____	windy	_____	_____

B. Look and write.

1. _____ was
   _____.

2. _____
   _____.

My Schedule

A. Read and write.

Mari and Sara are sisters.

1. They go to their English class on _____ and _____.

2. They go to their math class on _____ in the morning.

3. They go to _____ practice on Monday and Wednesday before school.

4. They go to _____ on Thursday _____.

🌸	Sunday	Monday	Tuesday	Wednesday	Thursday	Friday	Saturday
AM		Volleyball		Volleyball		Math Class	
PM	English		English		swimming		piano lesson

✓

My Town

A. Read and write the letter.

1. She sometimes helps animals. _____

2. He usually catches fish. _____

3. He usually fixes cars. _____

4. She always takes pictures. _____

B. Read and write.

What about you?

What do you see every day?

1. I always see _____ .

2. I usually see _____ .

3. I sometimes see _____ .

4. I never see _____ .

Sports

A. Look and write.

The _____
is taller than _____
_____
_____.

The _____
is _____
_____.

The _____
_____
than _____
_____.

B. Write. What about you?

Which sports do you like?

1. I like _____.

2. I don't like _____.

3. I like _____ more than

_____.